# MONTESSORI, WALDORF, TOGETHER

## A Toddler's Journey of Discovery

68 Activities to Foster Development, Creativity and Connection from 12-24 Months

# Table of contents

Introduction ....                                        1

For Motor Development...                                 3

For Language and Early Literacy...                      15

For Creative Play...                                    24

For Cognitive Development...                            39

For Bonding..                                           50

For Social and Emotional Development...                 53

For Nature Play...                                      58

For Sensory Play...                                     70

Thank You...                                            79

# INTRODUCTION

As you have probably discovered in the first magical years of your child's life, the early years are full of wonder, play, and fun - experiences that are rich in learning, growth and development. Seeing your child grow and develop skills has to be one of the biggest blessings you've ever been given. If you picked up this book, you likely know that your child's brain is in its most dramatic period of growth from birth until age five. Imagine seeing water falling out of the sky for the first time! Or noticing the smile on your mothers face - then recognising that the human it belongs to is yours! Play and discovery is your little one's greatest teacher during this time, and it is a very, very, powerful tool. Do NOT underestimate the one on one play time you have with your child, there is magic in these moments. They are learning through the world around them, soaking up everything like sponges through observation, and the experiences and environments you provide for them.

This year, in your child's second year of growth, you will start to notice your little one coming into their own, developing their personality and own little soul. There's so much to look forward to, as they grow from a baby, to a toddler. I know from experience that this is one of the most fascinating years, you will notice so many changes, over such a short period of time. In the year ahead, they will learn to walk, run, climb, sing, speak, scribble, interact more with friends and entertain themselves.

We created this book in the hopes that our play based learning prompts will make it easy for you to understand how to support your little ones early learning and development. I know that I was endlessly googling, finding resources, so I hoped to provide some answers all in one easy place. The other thing that I found, is that it's important for your toddler not to see you stuck to the screen, since they personally don't understand what it is you're looking at. Better for them to see you reading a book, am I right?

Our aim is to inspire you with a range of fun and simple, age and developmentally appropriate activities that you can easily do at home, outdoors somewhere nearby, in the local park - anywhere that doesn't require any special equipment. Montessori play is often focused on particular toys - but we don't feel that is necessary. We have put together both Waldorf and Montessori inspired activities - and to be honest, sometimes it is easy to get caught up in the jargon of the day. We just want to encourage the life-long love of learning, from anywhere, at any time. As an educator myself, I encourage you to adapt these activities as you see fit, tailor them to your child and situation. I educate my son at home who is now five, and we are often adapting lessons, going with the flow and seeing what fits best. I believe this is the best way to go about these ideas too.

So here are 68 ideas - more than one for each week of the year. Remember, the best development tool of all is to give your child loads of child-led free play! We encourage you to inspire it, not to control it.

For easy reference I have divided the prompts into specific areas of development including creativity, fine and gross motor skills, cognitive development, language and early literacy (though not too many here for this age - read, read, read!), sensory play, nature and outdoor play and social and emotional wellbeing.

To set up an activity, simply flick to a page you want to try and you think your toddler might enjoy, prepare any materials and invite them to join you! You may need to show your little one what to do, but then let them take the lead and watch the magic unfold. They may end up doing something completely different - but that is okay too, and actually, to be encouraged! Under your supervision let them play, play, play - and try not to control the outcome too much. Letting them explore their own ideas will foster in them a sense of autonomy and agency from a really young age and give them a much richer experience. If they're having fun, regardless of what the instructions say, they're doing it right.

If they enjoy the activity, you should DEFINITELY encourage them to do this regularly. Just like reading a regular book is encouraged, listening to similar songs over and over, so is repeating the activities. You could build some of these experiences into your daily routine. Invite your friends over to join you. Create your own little toddler club. Whoever has the biggest back garden, and can make the biggest mess - wins! Why not? Have fun with it. If built into your routine, the repetition of the activity at the same time each week, will provide a comforting sense of rhythm for your child - a cornerstone in Waldorf and Montessori philosophy.

# For Motor Development...

# Treasure Wall

Gather a few treasures, like ribbons, tiny toys, balls, some of their favourite things in different textures and sizes. Use tape to individually tape each item to the wall, at different heights. Encourage your little one to walk along the wall and remove and investigate each treasure. Talk about the colours, shapes, feel, size etc with them.

# Out to Dry

Tie a string between two table legs and help your child to peg up some socks from a laundry basket onto the makeshift washing line. They might pull them down, put them into the basket, put them back up again. You could have them do this as you hang out your own washing, they may wish to copy you.

# Push/Pull

Find a cardboard box, or a washing basket, and a bunch of soft toys and teddies that your toddler loves. Encourage them to put the toys into the box and take them on a fun adventure by pushing them around the house, balcony or up and down your street! You could use chalk or tape to make a track on the floor, or add a handle or some string and get them to pull the box. I once made a car out of an old milk carton, some string, tape and duplo wheels and we gave my son's favourite teddy hours of riding fun!

# Laundry Basketball

You don't even need real balls for this one, find a few pairs of socks and roll them into balls! Place the laundry basket close to your bub and show them how to throw the socks into the basket. You can gradually pull the basket further away as they improve or place it higher. Make sure you cheer excitedly when they get a 'goal!' - this one is a great lesson in persistence.

# Sticky Wall

Attach a sheet of transparent adhesive to the wall with the sticky side out - or if you need to get creative, you can make do with some masking tape folded over onto itself. Help your child to stick some lightweight items like bits of string, cotton balls or buds, leaves, feathers etc. Invite them to peel them off and put them into a bucket, which will help them to develop their little pincer grip.

# Obstacle Course

Create a simple obstacle course using pillows, cushions and soft toys. Encourage your toddler to crawl over, under, and through the obstacles, helping them to develop their coordination and balance. You can also create a tunnel, and put some items inside the tunnel for them to collect as they make their way to you!

# Stacking Towers

Use soft blocks or cups for your toddler to stack into towers, watch them use and develop their hand dexterity as they stack and knock down the towers.

# Finger Painting

Allow your toddler to explore finger painting with safe, washable paints. If you don't have any in the house, grab some flour, some food colouring, and get creative!

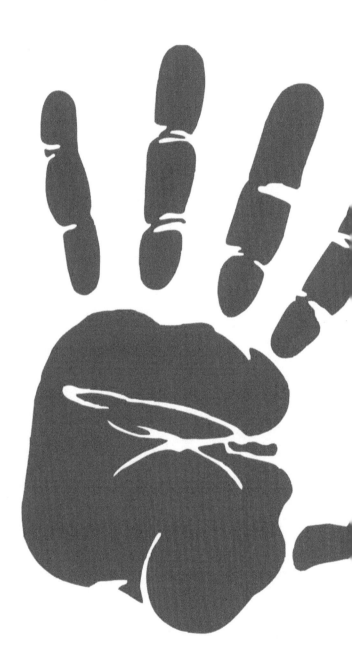

# Balloon Volleyball

If you have some leftover balloons from your most recent party, blow one up and use it as a volleyball, gently tossing it back and forth with your toddler. Be loud and fun, don't let it touch the ground, make a big deal out of it!

# Dance Party

This has to be one of my favourites and has definitely become part of our daily routine. You can download apps for children so that the song repetition is familiar. But just put on some music and have a dance party together, develop their rhythm and gross motor skills with fun!

# Water Play

Set up a shallow container of water and some fun toys, or cups, saucepans, anything you like! Let your toddler splash, pour and play with the water enhancing their hand coordination and sensory experiences.

# For Language and Literacy ...

# 3D Story Time

Choose a favourite book and choose some objects from outdoors and/or around the house to feature in the story. For example, you could use a scarf to represent a river, twigs for trees, toys for the characters. Interact with your child as you use the objects to enact the story and bring it to life.

# Shadow Stories

Shine the lamp on the wall in your room and use your hands to create stories using your own imagination, make ducks or other familiar animals to your bub. Encourage them to use their hands to do the same. My girl loves this game and we do it every single time we wake her up from nap time.

# Sing Nursery Rhymes

Sing familiar nursery rhymes with simple, repetitive lyrics. This helps toddlers develop their listening and vocabulary. We even started our own singing group in our local area and met twice a week to do this with our babies. Your local library may have a similar activity depending where you live. Be sure to include songs with actions like 'Head, Shoulders, Knees and Toes' or 'Wheels on the Bus'.

# Rhyme Time

Play a simple rhyming game by saying words that rhyme and encouraging your toddler to repeat them after you, like 'cat-hat' and 'dog-log'.

# Conversation time

Engage your toddler in simple conversations throughout the day. Describe what you are doing and ask open-ended questions like 'What did you do today?' or 'What is your favourite colour?' Make sure every time you are going to do something, you explain it to them. For example, don't just pick them up and put them in the car without explanation. Let them know where you are going, what you are doing, and chat to them on the way. I noticed my son's language developed really early and I think this was a big part of it.

## Name Game and Animal Sounds

Repeat your toddlers name and encourage them to say their own name. You can also name family members, objects and animals. Point to photographs of loved ones, or animal books and toys. Show them an animal in a book or with a toy, and mimic its sound. They love introducing new sounds into their vocabulary. My daughter is often snorting around the house with her toy pig.

# Sign Language

We learnt a lot of sign language and did this together at the same time as well, signs for food, milk, hungry, more etc. It was a lot of fun, and my 5 year old and I often still use signs together.

# Mirror Talk

Stand in front of the mirror with your toddler and make different facial expressions. Name the emotions that you are portraying like happy, sad, surprised. See what they come up with on their own.

For Creative
Play...

# Sound Hunt

Head outdoors with your toddler. Give them a pair of sticks and encourage them to tap things they find on the walk and see what sound they make. Creative musical games like this help your child attune their ear to the various musical tones in their environment whilst simultaneously piquing their curiosity about the world around them.

# On a Roll

Assist your child to paint some toilet roll tubes in bright colours. Once they are dry, show your little one how they can stack them into a pyramid formation. Observe what they do next. They may line the up, knock them down, squash them, look through them. Their ideas lead the way.

# Creature Feature

If your child is already familiar with some animal sounds and movements, they are ready for this fun game! Put on some upbeat music and call out names of different animals that match the tempo like dog, cat, mouse, kangaroo, rabbit. Join them in adopting the movements of each creature. Then slow the tempo and choose animals that match it like a koala or a sloth. This will be so much fun and encourage their sense of self.

# Loaf Tin Guitar

Find a loaf baking tin and some rubber bands. Help your child put the rubber bands onto the tin to make some 'guitar strings'. Show them how to play the instrument, and bring out some saucepan drums to play along and make songs together.

# Giants and Pixies

This is a fun dancing game to teach your child about size and volume. Find a loud piece of music, and a soft piece of music. Alternative between stomping like a giant to the heavy robust music, and tiptoeing like a pixie to the soft tunes. Let them take the lead, and you can demonstrate some corresponding big and small movements that match the volume.

# Let it Snow

Make snow domes by filling some old food jars with water and adding some different items like desiccated coconut for snow, other spices, flowers and seeds. Shake and upend the jar, and talk about the movement of the items as they float and fall.

# We Built This City

Deconstruct a couple of cardboard boxes and lay them flat, taped together. Draw a variety of roads and houses with a marker as you ask your toddler for suggestions (What can we see in a town? Who lives here? Whose house is that? Are there any animals?). Whilst they may not be able to offer much in the way of verbal responses, you are building their vocabulary and language skills every time you talk to them. Provide some toy cars or animal figurines, what you have already, for them to use with the homemade play mat.

# Nature Art

Deconstruct a couple of cardboard boxes and lay them flat, taped together. Draw a variety of roads and houses with a marker as you ask your toddler for suggestions (What can we see in a town? Who lives here? Whose house is that? Are there any animals?). Whilst they may not be able to offer much in the way of verbal responses, you are building their vocabulary and language skills every time you talk to them. Provide some toy cars or animal figurines, what you have already, for them to use with the homemade play mat.

# Bubble Wrap Stomp

Has a package arrived recently? We don't encourage buying bubble wrap, but if there is some around, let your toddler stomp on it, play with it, pop it. This is a fun tactile way to explore textures. Do so with other different things lying around the house before you throw them out.

# Follow the Leader

Take turns being the leader and have your toddler mimic your movements, or play a game of 'Mummy says' aka 'Simon Says'.

# Magic Wand and Potion Play

Pretend that sticks are magic wands. You can even decorate them with ribbon and beads. Use them to cast spells, make things disappear or turn objects into something else. Fill cups or containers with water and let your toddler mix in some food colouring to pretend they are making magic potions.

# Body Painting

Lay out a large sheet or paper to let your toddler explore painting their hands, feet and body. This is messy but lots of fun! Keep the prints for framing later - and be sure to take lots of pictures.

# Nesting

Set the context by showing your child some pictures of bird nests. You could talk about their shape, what they are made of, how they use them. Then make a bird's nest together by lawyering some mud, soft, or dry materials like yarn, features, dry leaves, old fabric, small twigs etc around a bowl. Leave it outside to dry and then remove it from the bowl, and help them to place it in a nearby bush for a bird to come and use.

# Marble Picasso

Head outside and fill two or three balloons with water so that they fit in your child's hands. Supply them with bowls of different coloured paint and a sheet of paper, or use the grass as their canvas! Encourage them to dip the balloons in the paint and decorate the canvas in any way they want to. You could use marbles instead. This messy, artistic free play gives your child a chance to let their imagination run wild and have lots of fun and make lots of mess.

# For Cognitive Development...

# Ramp it Up

Gather a variety of round and cylindrical objects such as a ball, orange, rolled up pair of socks, tin can, cardboard tube. Make a simple ramp by propping up a tray or chopping board and then show your child how to roll the objects down it. Let them check their predictions by trying to roll other objects too. Position your toddler at the bottom of the ramp afterwards and let them try to catch the objects.

# Food Find

Fill a bowl with dry cereal and bury some small foods for your toddler to find and eat like sultanas, finely diced food and vegetables. This is also a fun way to try new foods or make disliked foods more exciting!

# Peek-a-Boo

Play peek-a-boo by hiding your face behind your hands or a cloth and then revealing it with a big smile. You all know how... and it's so much fun to see the big grin on their faces.

# Sorting Games

Provide different types of safe objects like toys, blocks, books and encourage your toddler to sort them by colour, shape or size. Remember a lot of it might be a bit over their heads for now, but they are always, always taking it in.

# Point and Find

Ask your toddler to point to familiar objects around the room or in a book. Ask them to retrieve different objects for you. When they are correct, cheer excitedly!

# Make a Rainbow

Next time you're at the hardware store, collect a handful of paint sample cards with some basic colours your little one will recognise. Sort the cards into colour groups together and then help them arrange the cards into a rainbow shape, in any order you wish. Having knowledge of colour comes in really handy in many situations that your child will later be exposed to like a red flag for danger at the beach, or understanding traffic lights.

# Dialogue in the Dark

Exploring light and shadow enables children to appreciate the awe and wonder of the world around them and provides an environment where they can develop their natural curiosity. Take two torches/flashlights into a darkened room and shine them on the wall and ceiling. Draw circles and lines and encourage your little one to copy the movements of your light.

# How Things Work

Take your little one to visit each room in the house. Show them, and let them try, flicking a light switch, opening a door, sliding a latch, pushing a button, opening and closing a window. Activities like this that seem natural to us are fascinating to children and help develop new connections in their brain.

# Spider Web

Take a laundry basket and a ball of string. Weave the string back and forth through the holes to create a three dimensional spider web inside the basket. Add several toys underneath and see if you little one can retrieve them.

# Photo Puzzle

Grab some familiar photos from around the house and sit down with your little one. Say the names of familiar faces in the pictures like 'Nanna' or 'Mumma' and see if they can point to their loved one.

For Bonding...

# Pamper Bath

Illuminate your bathroom with candles, torches or a lamp. Put on some soft music and take a relaxing bubble bath together. Get your little one to pamper you by washing your hands and feet with a sponge and giving you a massage! Enjoy your special bonding time together.

# Camp Out

Build a fort or set up a tent in your back garden and fill it with comfy blankets and cushions. Snuggle in there together with a book, talk gently and intimately and encourage your bonding time. When you create a space that they love, chances are they'll want to stay there and connect with you.

# For Social and Emotional Development...

# Hi and Bye

Take your bub on an outing to the local shops and practice saying 'hello' as you enter a place, and 'goodbye' as you leave. Practising these greetings with your child will help them to develop their behaviour and build their confidence in meeting unfamiliar people.

# Encourage Sharing

During play, encourage your toddler to share toys or take turns with others. Praise and acknowledge their efforts. Learn the sign for 'share' and use this often.

# Is Anyone Home?

Make a house with a cardboard box, or simply hide behind your child's bedroom door. Role play knocking on the door, ringing the bell and asking if anyone is home. Another way my daughter likes to roleplay is by encouraging me to pretend to sleep (she indicates this with a snoring sound). After I do so, she jumps on me in delight and I pretend she has woken me up. Knock, knock!

# Give a Gift

Wrap some objects up in some fabric or old paper and allow your little one to unwrap them. You can do this with layers of different materials and talk about what is inside each layer. Encourage them to find a special gift and wrap it up for a family member or friend. They could even use their own artwork as the gift, or as the paper. This is a lovely way to encourage giving, receiving, and expressing gratitude.

For Nature
Play...

# Leaf Piles

During Autumn, gather lots of leaves using a rake (they can help!) and make a big pile for your toddler to play in. Let them jump, toss and explore the leaves. Show them how it's done!

# It's Raining, it's Pouring

Next time it rains, run out into it with your toddler!
Jump, laugh, lay down facing the sky. This never
fails to delight, and honestly, it's the best feeling in
the world for us as adults too. I find this really
meditative and can snap me out of any mood.

# Nature Scavenger Hunt

Create a simple scavenger hunt list with items like a rock, a leaf, a flower, and a stick. Have your toddler find these items on the outdoor adventure. Draw a map with pictures of where you might find the items and point to them as you do.

# Bug Exploration

Look for insects like ants, butterflies, ladybugs. Observe them together and discuss their shapes, movements, colours. If they show an interest, research the bugs when you get home. This was my son's favourite activity as a toddler and we still go 'bug hunting' each morning. He can tell you every single variety of praying mantis and millipede there is!

# Rock Painting

Collect some smooth rocks and paint them together. This is a wonderfully fun and artistic outdoor activity. Keep the rocks around your house or place them along walking paths in your local community for others to find.

# Nature Sounds

Sit quietly and listen to the sounds of birds chirping, wind rustling the leaves, water running, all of the natural sounds you can hear. Talk about what you hear quietly, and encourage listening really closely.

# Picnic Play

Have a picnic outdoors and let your toddler enjoy snacks surrounded by nature. This is a lovely experience for everyone involved. Let them wander off, as long as you have your eye on them, encourage them to explore.

# Planting Seeds

Plant some easy to grow seeds in your garden or a pot, and watch them grow together. Encourage watering each day, and a daily time to check on their progress. Discuss how plants grow and follow this process together.

# Worm Farm

When my son was younger, we ordered a worm farm kit. This was a wonderful way to explore nature inside, because we lived in an apartment and kept it on the balcony. They can be encouraged each day to water and turn the soil, and they may even like to hold the worms gently.

# Beach or Nature Shelf

Each time you go on a nature or beach walk, collect some new things like pine cones, crab claws, cuttlefish, seed pods, special leaves and rocks or shells. Ask your child to carry them home and make a nature table or shelf by labelling each of the items and placing them in their own special place. You don't have to be so specific, I know my son liked to place everything in a big messy bowl and occasionally take the items out to investigate.

# Nature Mask

Go on a nature walk together and look for the biggest leaf you can find. Bring it home, cut out some eye holes and paint it (if you like) to make a mask. Show your child how they can use the stem to hold the mask in front of their face and peek through the eye holes.

# For Sensory Play...

# Rainbow Rice Bin

Dye rice or pasta with different colours using food colouring, and let your toddler scoop, pour, and explore the different colours with their hands or cups and spoons. They can even sort the colours, or just explore the textures. Do the whole process together, including the dying so they can be included in it all.

# Cloud Dough

Mix flour and baby oil to create a soft, moldable texture. Let your toddler shape and squish the cloud dough.

# Edible Sensory Play

Offer safe, edible sensory materials like cooked pasta, oatmeal, or cooked and cooled jello for your toddler to touch and explore. Put different textures in different tupperware containers and place them out on the grass. Mine usually ends up eating half of it but it's so much fun.

# Gel Sensory Bags

Fill sealable plastic bags with hair gel or a similar substance and add small toys or items. Seal the bags and let your toddler press and manipulate the contents.

# Foam Play

Fill a container with whipped cream for your toddler to play with. They can draw in the foam and make squiggles. You could use shaving cream, just be careful they don't eat it like mine would!

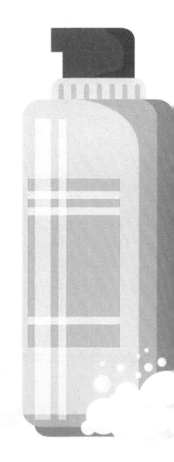

# Ice Play

Freeze small toys or objects in water and let your toddler use warm water to melt the ice and uncover the hidden items. Start the process with them by including them in the freezing process too.

# Flower Power Perfume

Make a variety of flower 'perfumes' by filling old bottles or jars with water, flowers, herbs, cinnamon, vanilla essence or rosewater. Talk to your little one about how each one smells and let them enjoy this sensory experience.

# Sand Play

If you have access to a beach or sandbox, children can play for hours with sand. Add some water and let your child create and play freely. Get cookie cutters and buckets involved. They may like to make castles, or decorate some 'sand cookies' with twigs, glitter, or whatever you have on hand.

Thank you so much for purchasing this book, and for investing time into your little one's development. We hope you enjoyed the activities, and would love it if you could share your positive experience with a review so that other parents can find us too.

Please feel free to send me an email to add yourself to the email list - or to just say hi. We are currently developing similar books for children aged 3 and 4, and absolutely love it when we hear from you. Enjoy this special time with your beautiful little soul.

Love, Brooke

Made in the USA
Las Vegas, NV
28 December 2024

15530736R00046